Level B

Shoreview, Minnesota

AMP™ *QReads*™ is based upon the instructional routine developed by **Elfrieda (Freddy) H. Hiebert** (Ph.D., University of Wisconsin—Madison). Professor Hiebert is Adjunct Professor at the University of California, Berkeley and has been a classroom teacher, university-based teacher, and educator for over 35 years. She has published over 130 research articles and chapters in journals and books on how instruction and materials influence reading acquisition. Professor Hiebert's TExT model for accessible texts has been used to develop widely-used reading programs, including *QuickReads*® and *QuickReads*® *Technology* (Pearson Learning Group).

The publisher wishes to thank the following educators for their helpful comments during the review process for *AMP*™ *QReads*™. Their assistance has been invaluable:

Shelley Al-Khatib, Teacher, Life Skills, Chippewa Middle School, North Oaks, MN; **Ann Ertl,** ESL Department Lead, Champlin Park High School, Champlin, MN; **Dr. Kathleen Sullivan,** Supervisor, Reading Services Center, Omaha Public Schools, Omaha, NE; **Ryan E. Summers,** Teacher, English, Neelsville Middle School, Germantown, MD.

Acknowledgments appear on page 176, which constitutes an extension of this copyright page.

ISBN-13: 978-0-7854-6303-0
ISBN-10: 0-7854-6303-8

1 2 3 4 5 6 7 8 9 10   11 10 09 08 07

1-800-992-0244
www.agsglobe.com

CONTENTS

Social Studies

Literature and Language

Science

Arts and Culture

Welcome to QReads™!

Please follow these steps for each page of readings:

FIRST READ

1. Read the Fast Facts and think about what you might already know about the topic. Look for two words that are new or difficult. Draw a line under these words.

2. Read the page aloud or silently to yourself. Always include the title at the top of the same page. Take as much time as you need.

3. Find the first page in Building Connections. Write some words or phrases there to help you remember what is important.

SECOND READ

1. Listen and read along silently with your teacher or the audio track.

2. Use the target rate of 1 minute when listening and reading along.

3. Ask yourself, what is one thing to remember? Answer the Key Notes question to help find what is important.

THIRD READ

1. Now, try to read as much of the page as you can within 1 minute.

2. Read silently as you are timed for 1 minute. Read aloud with a partner or your teacher. Circle the last word you read at the end of 1 minute.

3. Write down the number of words you read on the page. Review in your mind what is important to remember.

4. Complete the questions or other reading given by your teacher.

National Symbols

The Statue of Liberty is in New York Harbor.

Fast Facts

- The first U.S. flag was approved by Congress on June 14, 1777.

- The Statue of Liberty is a symbol of freedom in the United States.

- In the United States, people say a pledge to the flag in which they promise to be true to their country.

Symbols of the United States

You have seen the flag flying at your school. You can see pictures of the bald eagle on money. The flag and the[28] bald eagle are symbols of the United States. When people see these symbols, they think about things that are important to the country.[51]

Freedom was important to the people who started this country. They wanted freedom for everyone. When people[68] who live in the United States see symbols like the flag or the bald eagle, they think about things that are important to them, like freedom.[94]

KEY NOTES

Symbols of the United States
What do people think when they see symbols of the United States?

_____

_____

National Symbols

The stars and stripes on the U.S. flag are symbols.

Fast Facts

- The U.S. flag is flown all day and night in the nation's capital.

- The last star was added to the flag when Hawaii became the 50th state.

- Every nation in the world has its own flag.

Stars and Stripes

Sometimes the flag of the United States is called the Stars and Stripes. A look at the flag will tell you why. Each [26] star on the flag stands for a state in the United States. Every time a new state was added to the United States, a star was added to the flag. The flag now has 50 stars. [62]

There are also 13 stripes on the flag. The number of stripes stays the same. The stripes stand for the areas that became the first 13 states in the United States. [93]

KEY NOTES

Stars and Stripes
Why is the U.S. flag called the Stars and Stripes?

_____

_____

National Symbols

Red, white, and blue is everywhere on July 4th.

Fast Facts

- The U.S. flag has changed its pattern, but it has never changed its colors.

- The red on the U.S. flag stands for strength, the white stands for purity, and the blue stands for justice.

- Every nation has colors that are important to its history.

Red, White, and Blue

If you like a sports team, you know that the team wears certain colors. Colors can also be symbols. People who want to show they like a sports team wear the colors of that team.[39]

The colors red, white, and blue are symbols of the United States. These are the colors on the U.S. flag. On July[61] 4th, people in the United States fly red, white, and blue flags on their houses. People also wear red, white, and blue on July 4th to show they love the United States.[93]

KEY NOTES
Red, White, and Blue How can colors be symbols? _____ _____

National Symbols

The bald eagle is a national symbol.

Fast Facts

- The bald eagle became the national bird of the United States in 1782.

- The bald eagle is the only eagle belonging to North America and no other place.

- The bald eagle can be found along rivers and large lakes.

Bald Eagle

The bald eagle is a bird that is a symbol of the United States. It was picked as a symbol because it is a strong and[28] beautiful bird. The bald eagle is not really bald, though. The white feathers on its head make it look bald. The rest of its feathers are dark.[55]

People used to hunt bald eagles. In the 1970s, there were not many bald eagles left. Laws were passed to keep bald[77] eagles safe. Now, there are four times as many bald eagles as there were in the 1970s.[94]

KEY NOTES

Bald Eagle

What does the bald eagle show about the United States?

_____

_____

National Symbols

Symbols of the United States

1. The main idea of "Symbols of the United States" is that _____

    a. the U.S. flag has a bald eagle on it.
    b. every country needs a flag.
    c. the bald eagle is the most important symbol of the United States.
    d. symbols make us think about things that are important.

2. What is a symbol?

_____

_____

_____

3. What two symbols of the United States did you learn about in this reading?

_____

_____

_____

Stars and Stripes

1. Another good name for "Stars and Stripes" is _____

    a. "Fifty States."
    b. "Our Country's Flag."
    c. "Stars in the Flag."
    d. "The Many States of the United States."

2. What do the stars and stripes on the flag stand for?

_____

_____

_____

3. What would happen to the U.S. flag if a new state were added?

    a. A new red stripe would be added.
    b. A new white stripe would be added.
    c. A new star would be added.
    d. The flag would stay the same.

Red, White, and Blue

1. "Red, White, and Blue" is MAINLY about _____

    a. why sports teams wear certain colors.
    b. what people do on July 4th.
    c. the colors red, white, and blue as symbols of the United States.
    d. the many different symbols of the United States.

2. List two facts you learned in "Red, White, and Blue."

_____

_____

_____

3. Why do people wear red, white, and blue on July 4th?

_____

_____

_____

Bald Eagle

1. Why was the bald eagle picked as a symbol of the United States?

    a. It is a strong and beautiful bird.

    b. It has blue and white feathers.

    c. It is the most famous bird in the United States.

    d. It is only found in the United States.

2. Why were laws passed about bald eagles in the 1970s?

_____

_____

_____

3. What happened to the bald eagle between the 1970s and today?

_____

_____

_____

symbols	eagle	July	1970s
freedom	colors	4th	feathers

1. Choose the word from the word box above that best matches each definition. Write the word on the line below.

   A. _____ things that stand for other things

   B. _____ the years between 1970 and 1979

   C. _____ a large bird

   D. _____ a month in the year

   E. _____ a number that comes after 3rd and before 5th

   F. _____ being able to do what you want to do

   G. _____ words that tell about how things look; red and white are examples

   H. _____ things that cover a bird's body

2. Fill in the blanks in the sentences below. Choose the word from the word box that completes each sentence.

   A. My father went to school during the years called the

   _____.

   B. The uniforms of Matt's favorite soccer team use the _____ blue and red.

   C. People in the United States have the _____ to say what they wish.

   D. _____ is one of the months in the summer.

   E. The flag and the bald eagle are _____ of the United States.

   F. The _____ on birds' wings help them fly.

   G. The _____ has large wings and can fly for a long time.

   H. July _____ is the day after July 3rd.

National Symbols

1. Use the idea web to help you remember what you read. In each box, write the main idea of that reading.

Symbols of the United States

_____

_____

_____

_____

Stars and Stripes

_____

_____

_____

_____

National Symbols

Red, White, and Blue

_____

_____

_____

_____

Bald Eagle

_____

_____

_____

_____

2. Tell about two symbols of the United States.

_____

_____

_____

_____

3. Which symbol do you think is the best symbol for the United States? Why?

_____

_____

_____

_____

4. Why do countries have national symbols like birds and flags?

_____

_____

_____

_____

Money

Long ago, people traded things and did not use money.

Rue des Archives / The Granger Collection, NYC

Fast Facts

- Both 1-dollar and 50-dollar bills cost the same to print.

- The leaders of a country decide how much that country's money is worth.

- If money loses its worth, people go back to trading things.

What Is Money?

Today, we use money to pay for the things we need or want. We get money when we are paid for doing something[26] or when we sell something. Long ago, people did not use money like we do today. They traded things. If one person[48] had food and another person had a rug, the food might be traded for the rug.[64]

Sometimes we still trade things like food and rugs. However, most times we do another kind of trading. We trade paper money for the things we want or need.[93]

KEY NOTES
What Is Money?
What can people do to get food or things they need or want?

_____

_____

Money

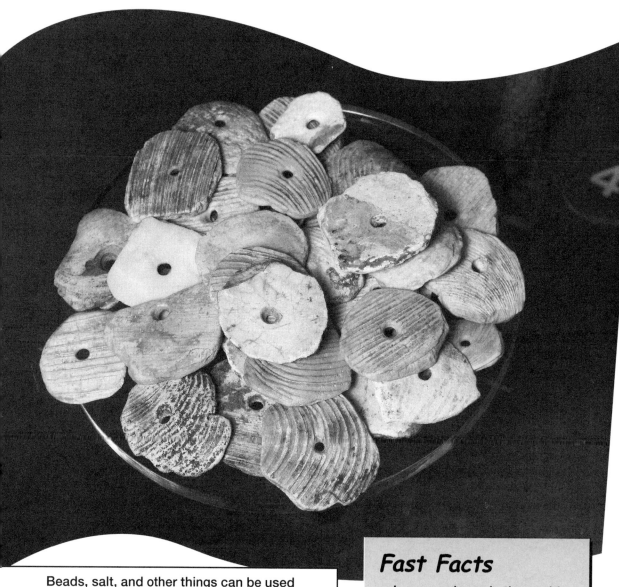

Beads, salt, and other things can be used as money.

Fast Facts

- In some places in the world, cows are used as money.

- The word *salary*, or money paid for doing a job, comes from the word *salt*.

- Anything can be used as money if everyone in a place agrees to it.

Different Kinds of Money

People have used different things for money. On one island, people used big stones as money. If what they wanted [24] cost a lot, they had to roll more than one stone to the person who was selling things. [42]

On another island, people used red feathers for money. Feathers that were redder were worth more than feathers that were less red. [64]

Long ago, salt was worth a lot. In some places, people used bars of salt as money. In the United States, the earliest people used beads as money. [92]

KEY NOTES

Different Kinds of Money

Why might people use different things for money?

_____

_____

Money

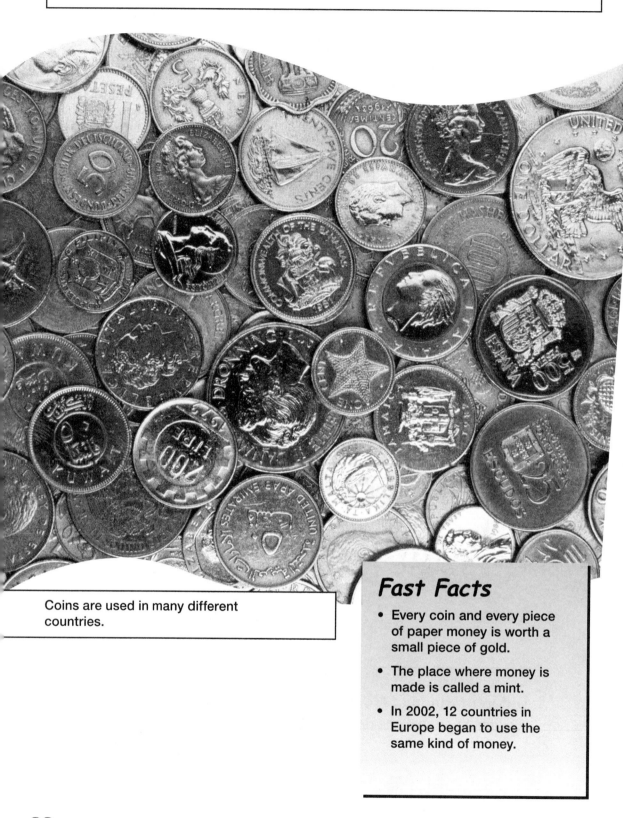

Coins are used in many different countries.

Fast Facts

- Every coin and every piece of paper money is worth a small piece of gold.

- The place where money is made is called a mint.

- In 2002, 12 countries in Europe began to use the same kind of money.

Coins and Paper Money

Many people used gold and silver to buy things. People would weigh the gold or silver to see how much they were[26] worth before using them. Weighing takes time, so people started making coins. The marks on the coins told people how much the coins were worth.[51]

Coins can weigh a lot. Also, it was not always safe to carry coins, so people left them at stores. Store owners gave their[75] customers notes that said the customers had left coins at the store. These notes were the first paper money.[94]

KEY NOTES

Coins and Paper Money
How did people use coins and paper money long ago?

_____

_____

Money

A bank card is useful, but it is not the same as money.

Fast Facts

- Computers can keep track of lost bank cards.

- Some banks let people pay back their money slowly, a little at a time.

- Some bank cards allow people to take out paper money from computers called ATMs.

Bank Cards

Today, many people don't carry a lot of coins or paper money. Instead, they use bank cards. Bank cards are small[23] plastic cards that computers can read. Computers tell banks to pay store owners for what people buy. Computers also tell[43] banks how much people need to pay to banks for what they have bought.[57]

Plastic bank cards are useful because people don't have to carry much money around with them. However, bank cards[76] are not money. People need to pay the bank for the things they have bought at a store.[94]

KEY NOTES

Bank Cards
Why do people use bank cards?

_____

_____

Money

What Is Money?

1. Before there was money, how did people pay for things?

    a. They sold things.
    b. They made their own things.
    c. They took what they needed.
    d. They traded things.

2. How do people use paper money today?

_____

_____

_____

3. Where do people today get the money for the things they want or need?

_____

_____

_____

Different Kinds of Money

1. "Different Kinds of Money" is MAINLY about _____

    a. the different things people have used for money.
    b. the big stones found on some islands.
    c. how people trade for things with money.
    d. how people use salt on their food.

2. Name three things that have been used for money.

_____

_____

_____

3. Why would red feathers be used for money?

    a. Red feathers could be found near the place.
    b. Red feathers were easier to weigh.
    c. Few red feathers could be found.
    d. There were lots of different colored feathers.

Coins and Paper Money

1. Why did people make gold and silver into coins?

    a. Gold and silver were easier to weigh than feathers.
    b. People wanted to see their money.
    c. Gold and silver took time to weigh.
    d. People found lots of gold and silver.

2. The first paper money told how much _____

    a. money a person owed to a store.
    b. a person could sell.
    c. money a person had left at a store.
    d. a person's coins weighed.

3. Why did people begin using paper money?

_____

_____

_____

Bank Cards

1. What are bank cards?

    a. paper money that people buy at a store
    b. plastic cards that people can use to buy things
    c. computers that give people money
    d. plastic cards that a person can buy at a store

2. How do people use bank cards?

_____

_____

_____

3. How are bank cards and paper money different?

_____

_____

_____

| trade | island | weigh | plastic |
| feathers | coins | silver | computers |

1. Choose the word from the word box above that best matches each definition. Write the word on the line below.

A. _____ small hard pieces of money

B. _____ things people use to work, send e-mail, or play games

C. _____ the soft coverings on a bird's body

D. _____ a small area of land with water around it

E. _____ something that can be hard to break and is used to make things

F. _____ something that can be used to make coins and watches

G. _____ to give something to someone and get something in return

H. _____ to find out how heavy something is

2. Fill in the blanks in the sentences below. Choose the word from the word box that completes each sentence.

A. The man will _____ the fish before he sells it.

B. The bright coins are made of _____ .

C. I needed a _____ bag to carry my gym clothes home.

D. Jose went to an _____ so he could lie on the beach.

E. _____ help birds stay warm and help them fly.

F. John and Lori do their work on _____ at school.

G. Mary used a few _____ to buy some gum.

H. Dan wanted to _____ some DVDs with Marta.

Money

What Is Money?

_____

_____

_____

_____

Different Kinds of Money

_____

_____

_____

_____

Money

Coins and Paper Money

_____

_____

_____

_____

Bank Cards

_____

_____

_____

_____

2. What is money?

_____

_____

_____

_____

3. Why was it important for money to weigh the right amount?

_____

_____

_____

_____

4. How is the money people use today different from the money people used long ago?

_____

_____

_____

_____

Cars: Then and Now

Early cars took the place of horses.

Fast Facts

- Steam vehicles were so heavy they went only 2 miles per hour.

- In 1908, Henry Ford made gas-engine cars costing $850. They were painted black because black paint cost less.

- Ford's Model T car went 35 miles per hour.

Car History

Over time, people have tried many ways to help them get from place to place. They have built vehicles run by horses,[24] wind, clocks, and steam. Yet these vehicles did not work well enough. People still wanted better, faster vehicles that did not cost a lot.[48]

In the 1800s, a vehicle was built that answered this wish—a car with a gas engine. Gas engines made cars easy to use[72] and fast. By the early 1900s, cars also cost less, so many people could buy them. The age of cars had begun.[94]

KEY NOTES

Car History

How have cars changed over time?

_____

_____

Cars: Then and Now

New cars are designed for safety.

Fast Facts

- The top colors for cars today are silver, black, and blue.

- The wheels on cars today are made to keep cars safe in all weather.

- Most cars today cost about $30,000, but a few cost nearly $400,000!

Today's Cars

Like older cars, most of today's cars work well and run on gas. However, many changes have been made in car design.[24] Two design areas—comfort and safety—have seen the most change.[35]

Cars today have parts made for comfort. Some parts make cars warm on a cold day and cool on a hot day. Some parts make cars turn more smoothly and engines sound softer.[68]

Cars today also place safety first. They are designed to stop more quickly. They also have air bags and seatbelts that keep people safe.[92]

KEY NOTES

Today's Cars
How are cars today different from older cars?

_____

_____

Cars: Then and Now

This car engine runs on a battery, not gas.

Fast Facts

- Some energy-saving cars cost more to run than gas cars.

- Electric cars keep the air about 97% cleaner than gas cars do, and they make little noise.

- Cars that run on electricity and gas can turn off their engine at a red light.

Energy-Saving Cars

Today, almost half a billion families around the world own cars. Most of these cars run on gas. This fact has caused[25] problems. First, gas is getting harder to find and it costs more. Second, gas makes air bad for living things.[45]

So, cars are being designed that use other kinds of energy. Some cars use energy from the Sun. Some use electricity.[66] Electric engines get their energy from batteries. Some cars use both gas and electricity. When these cars speed up, they save gas by running on their battery.[93]

KEY NOTES

Energy-Saving Cars
What are energy-saving cars?

_____

_____

Cars: Then and Now

Race cars are designed for racing on tracks.

Fast Facts

- People began to race cars in the 1800s.

- There are many different kinds of race cars and races, including hill climbing, city to city, and open wheel.

- In the United States, races are usually run on tracks shaped like an oval.

Race Cars

People today race cars for fun and for money. They want to show that their car is the fastest one. Many people also like to watch others race cars.[31]

Some race cars look like everyday cars. However, they were designed just for racing. Everything on them—from their wheels to their engine—has been changed.[57]

Race cars run on closed roads called tracks. Tracks have special designs. Certain kinds of race cars do better on certain[78] tracks. For example, a car with a big engine runs better on a shorter track.[93]

KEY NOTES

Race Cars
What are race cars?

_____

_____

Cars: Then and Now

Car History

1. "Car History" is MAINLY about _____

    a. how cars were first built.
    b. why people used horses.
    c. thc kinds of vehicles that were built.
    d. getting from place to place.

2. Name two problems with the first vehicles.

_____

_____

_____

3. What kind of engine changed car history? How?

_____

_____

_____

Today's Cars

1. Cars today have had many changes in their _____

    a. colors.
    b. design.
    c. shape.
    d. drivers.

2. What are two things that make today's cars more comfortable?

_____

_____

_____

3. Name two ways that cars are safer today.

_____

_____

_____

Energy-Saving Cars

1. Another good name for "Energy-Saving Cars" is _____

    a. "Why People Own Lots of Cars."
    b. "Why Gas Is Bad."
    c. "Why Energy-Saving Cars Cost More."
    d. "Cars That Solve Problems."

2. Name two types of energy-saving cars.

_____

_____

_____

3. What are two reasons people have made energy-saving cars?

_____

_____

_____

Race Cars

1. In this reading, the word *race* means _____

   a. a road that is closed to drivers.
   b. a car that goes fast on tracks.
   c. a way to find the fastest car.
   d. cars that run on gas.

2. How are race cars different from everyday cars?

_____

_____

_____

3. Why might people like to watch cars race?

_____

_____

_____

vehicle	engine	design	comfort
safety	energy	electric	battery

1. Choose the word from the word box above that best matches each definition. Write the word on the line below.

A. _____ something used to carry people and things, like a car

B. _____ the way something is planned

C. _____ electric power that can make cars and other things run

D. _____ something that makes life easier

E. _____ relating to a kind of energy you can get from batteries and wall plugs

F. _____ freedom from harm

G. _____ power that can be used to move something or someone

H. _____ a motor that makes things run

2. Fill in the blanks in the sentences below. Choose the word from the word box that completes each sentence.

A. A car is one kind of _____. Other kinds are trucks and trains.

B. I like the _____ of my own room because it is warm and quiet.

C. I had to charge the _____ for eight hours.

D. Electric cars get their _____ from a battery.

E. The most important _____ rule is to look both ways before crossing the street.

F. The new car _____ has shaded windows and more tail lights.

G. My car's _____ is large, so the car can go very fast.

H. Joan wants to save gas, so she bought an _____ car.

Cars: Then and Now

1. Use the idea web to help you remember what you read. In each box, write the main idea of that reading.

Car History

_____

_____

_____

_____

Today's Cars

_____

_____

_____

_____

Cars: Then and Now

Energy-Saving Cars

_____

_____

_____

_____

Race Cars

_____

_____

_____

_____

2. How have cars changed since they were first made?

_____

_____

_____

_____

3. How do you think the first cars changed the way people lived?

_____

_____

_____

_____

4. Name two ways that today's cars can be different from each other.

_____

_____

_____

_____

Writing About Oneself

Some people write about their feelings in a diary.

Fast Facts

- A soldier's diary from the American Revolution sold for $64,000.

- Leonardo da Vinci drew designs for flying machines in his diary—hundreds of years before airplanes were invented.

- A famous diary in the 1660s was 3,000 pages.

Writing for Yourself

Some people like to write in books that are called diaries. They might write about feelings that they want[22] to keep private, or not share with anyone. Diary writers might write about a problem they have that is hard to[43] talk about. They might write things they can't even tell a friend.[55]

Although some people use diaries to write about feelings and thoughts that they want to keep private,[72] other people write about the world around them. For these people, writing in diaries can be a way to think[92] about and understand things that happen and people they meet.[102]

KEY NOTES

Writing for Yourself
What is a diary?

_____

_____

Writing About Oneself

Anne Frank's diary has been read by millions of people.

Fast Facts

- Anne Frank's diary was a present for her thirteenth birthday, just weeks before she went into hiding.

- Anne's father, Otto, was the only person in the group who survived the war.

- More than 25 million copies of Anne Frank's diary have been sold.

Anne Frank's Diary

Some people keep diaries that tell about their thoughts. Anne Frank kept this kind of diary while her[21] family and four other people hid from the Nazis during World War II.[34]

Anne wrote about the war, about growing up, and about living in a small space with many people. She[53] thought of her diary as a friend that she could talk to about anything. Anne wrote, "When I write, I can shake off all my cares."[79]

In 1944, two years after Anne and the others began hiding, the Nazis found them. Anne died in a Nazi camp in 1945.[102]

KEY NOTES

Anne Frank's Diary
What did Anne Frank write about?

_____

_____

Writing About Oneself

This is a painting showing the Great Fire of London.

Fast Facts

- The Great Fire lasted for five days.

- A large part of London was burned in the Great Fire, including 13,200 houses and 87 churches.

- After the Great Fire, houses in London were built of brick or stone, not wood, to make them fireproof.

Writing About the World

Some people keep diaries that tell about the world around them. In the 1660s, Samuel Pepys kept a diary[23] about what was happening in the city of London. Pepys's diary tells about what people saw and did in London in the 1600s.[46]

Pepys also wrote about the Great Fire of London, which burned much of the city in 1666. He wrote about[66] the fire spreading through the city and about people trying to save their things. Because Samuel Pepys kept[84] a diary, we know a lot about the Great Fire of London and what life was like in the 1600s.[104]

KEY NOTES

Writing About the World
What did Pepys write about?

_____

_____

Writing About Oneself

A blog is a diary that people share with others.

Fast Facts

- The first blog was posted in 1995.

- In 2005, more people in the United States posted blogs than did people in any other country.

- Between 10 million and 32 million people in the United States read blogs.

Writing a Blog

The Internet has made possible a special kind of diary called a blog. The word *blog* is made from the words *Web* and *log*.[27]

Blogs are different from the usual diaries because blogs aren't private. Anyone who goes on the Internet[44] can read a blog. Some blogs are also different from other diaries because others can write in them, too.[63] People might wish to start a conversation with anyone who visits their blog. They hope that others will join[82] their conversation, posting their ideas and opinions. In this way, people can learn about the opinions of others from around the world.[104]

KEY NOTES

Writing a Blog
What is a blog?

_____

_____

Writing About Oneself

Writing for Yourself

1. Another good name for "Writing for Yourself" is _____

    a. "Writing About the Past."
    b. "Keeping a Diary."
    c. "Why Friends Are Important."
    d. "Diaries I Have Read."

2. What is the main idea of "Writing for Yourself"?

    a. to tell you what to write in your diary
    b. to tell about important diaries
    c. to tell why people write in diaries
    d. to tell about something that is private

3. Why do people write in diaries?

_____

_____

_____

Anne Frank's Diary

1. This passage is MAINLY about _____

    a. what happened in World War II to Anne Frank.
    b. the Nazis in World War II.
    c. Anne Frank's family.
    d. what was in Anne Frank's diary.

2. Explain your answer to question 1.

_____

_____

_____

3. Why do you think many people read Anne Frank's diary?

_____

_____

_____

Writing About the World

1. Another good name for "Writing About the World" is _____

    a. "The Great Fire of London."
    b. "Life in London."
    c. "Fires of the 1600s."
    d. "Diaries About the World."

2. What can people learn from reading the diary of Samuel Pepys?

_____

_____

_____

3. What is the main idea of "Writing About the World"?

   a. We can learn about other times and places in diaries.
   b. The Great Fire of London was very bad.
   c. London is much safer today than in the 1600s.
   d. Samuel Pepys loved writing about his life in London.

Writing a Blog

1. In this reading, *opinions* means _____

   a. what people think is funny.
   b. the news.
   c. what people think about something.
   d. how to do something.

2. How are blogs different from the usual diaries?

_____

_____

_____

3. How is posting on a blog like having a conversation?

_____

_____

_____

diary	Samuel Pepys	opinions	Nazis
private	blog	conversation	London

1. Choose a word from the word box above that best matches each definition. Write the word on the line below.

A. _____ a person who wrote a famous diary in the 1600s

B. _____ your ideas and thoughts

C. _____ something that you don't want to share with others

D. _____ a book in which you write about your life

E. _____ people who came to power during World War II

F. _____ talking to someone

G. _____ a diary posted on the Web

H. _____ a city in England

2. Fill in the blanks in the sentences below. Choose the word from the word box that completes each sentence.

A. Marcos wanted to keep his writings _____.

B. I don't let anyone read my _____.

C. When the _____ came to power, the Frank family hid.

D. I would love to take a trip to the city of _____.

E. My _____ lists the songs I like most.

F. To learn about the Great Fire, we read what _____ wrote about it.

G. I have strong _____ about what things I want to wear.

H. I had a long _____ with my best friend.

Writing About Oneself

1. Using the diagram below, list how blogs and other diaries are different and alike. In the area where the circles overlap, list ways in which blogs and diaries are alike. In the area where the circles do not overlap, list ways in which blogs and diaries are different.

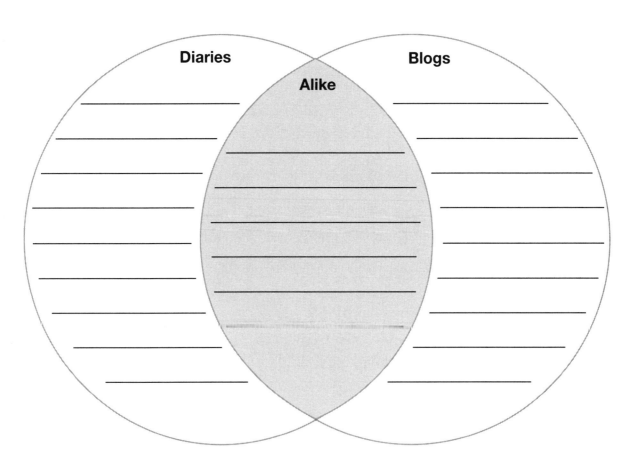

2. Write a short blog about yourself that you might post on the Web.

_____

_____

_____

_____

3. If you could read a diary or a blog that was written by a famous person, whose diary or blog would you pick? Explain your choice.

_____

_____

_____

_____

4. Have you ever kept a diary or a blog? Why or why not? Explain.

_____

_____

_____

_____

How the News Gets to You

Reading newspapers is one way to learn about the news.

Fast Facts

- Japan has the newspaper with the most readers: 14,532,694.

- In the United States, people can read more than 4,000 newspapers on the Web.

- Around the world, almost 1 billion people use the Web.

Choices in the News

Long ago, people learned about the news by seeing something happen or talking to others. Today, you can learn[23] what's happening by reading newspapers or Web sites. You can also hear the news on radio or TV.[41]

Newspapers run hundreds of stories that tell more than just the main facts. Many stories run on the Web, too, but most people read only the first page they see.[71]

Radio and TV news may run every hour, but they tell only about a few stories. Like Web sites, though, radio and TV stories can be changed as quickly as the news changes.[104]

KEY NOTES

Choices in the News

What are three different ways you can learn about the news today?

_____

_____

_____

How the News Gets to You

A reporter asks about something that happened.

Fast Facts

- In 1930, Dorothy Knapp became one of the first women reporters on TV.

- In 2004, there were 52,730 newspaper reporters working in the United States.

- In 2004, more than 20,000 women worked for newspapers.

Reporting the News

Reporters find out the news. They ask who, what, why, when, where, and how something happened. Reporters may[21] report on a fire in your town, a new law that may be passed, or a war in another country.[41]

No matter where their stories run, though, all reporters work in the same way. They talk to people who have seen[62] something happen. They talk to or even travel with the police to learn about crimes. Some travel with the army to report on[85] wars. These reporters sometimes put their lives in danger to tell people what is happening around the world.[103]

KEY NOTES

Reporting the News
How do reporters find out the news?

_____

_____

How the News Gets to You

News photographers go where news is happening.

Fast Facts

- Mathew Brady and his staff took more than 7,000 pictures of the Civil War.

- In 2002, about 130,000 people in the United States worked as photographers.

- In 2005, a photograph called "The Kiss," which was taken in France in 1945, sold for more than $200,000.

Seeing the News

Photographs show the *who* and the *where* of the news. Photographers, or people who take pictures, go to where the[23] news happens. Then, they take photographs or movies that show others what they saw. Their photographs or movies can[42] affect how people think about the people and events that are in the news.[56]

For example, some photographs taken in the 1960s showed people in the South who were being hurt by unfair laws.[76] These photographs affected how people felt about others' rights, and they helped get laws changed. Photographs have also affected how people feel about wars.[100]

KEY NOTES

Seeing the News

How do photographs help people learn about the news?

_____

_____

How the News Gets to You

Ida B. Wells was a teacher and a reporter.

Fast Facts

- Ida B. Wells's mother and father were born into slavery.

- Wells wanted women to have the same rights as men.

- In 1884, Wells sat in a whites-only part of a train to fight for African Americans' rights.

Ida B. Wells Reports

In 1884, Ida B. Wells was a teacher in the South. She was also a newspaper reporter who wrote about African[25] Americans. Wells wrote that African Americans did not have the same rights as white people. When she wrote that her city[46] did not give African American schools enough money, she lost her teaching job.[59]

Next, Wells bought part of a newspaper. When she wrote about African Americans who were killed by whites, a white[79] group broke her printing press and said she would be killed. Although Wells moved to another city, she never stopped reporting on African Americans' rights.[104]

KEY NOTES

Ida B. Wells Reports

What did Ida B. Wells report about?

_____

_____

How the News Gets to You

Choices in the News

1. "Choices in the News" is MAINLY about _____

    a. when radio and TV news change.
    b. different ways to find out about the news.
    c. how to find the news on Web sites.
    d. why people read the news in newspapers.

2. Long ago, how did people learn about the news?

    a. by seeing something happen or talking to others
    b. by reading the news on Web sites
    c. by hearing the radio or watching TV
    d. by talking to people who wrote newspapers

3. What are two differences between the news in newspapers and on the radio?

_____

_____

_____

Reporting the News

1. What is a reporter?

    a. someone who prints newspapers
    b. someone who finds out about the news
    c. someone who makes laws about the news
    d. someone who travels with the police

2. Tell about two ways reporters learn about the news.

_____

_____

_____

3. What are three things reporters want to find out about news stories?

_____

_____

_____

Seeing the News

1. The main idea of "Seeing the News" is that _____

    a. people can learn more from photographs than from news stories.
    b. photographs can help readers learn more about the news.
    c. news stories need photographs so people can understand them.
    d. photographers take many pictures for every story.

2. In this reading, _affect_ means _____

    a. to cause something or someone to change.
    b. to see something that has happened.
    c. to take a clear photograph for a story.
    d. to show the _who_ and the _where_ of the news.

3. How can photographs affect how people think about the news?

_____

_____

_____

Ida B. Wells Reports

1. Which of the following is NOT a fact about Ida B. Wells?

    a. She was a teacher.
    b. She wrote about white people's rights.
    c. She was a newspaper owner.
    d. She wrote about African Americans' rights.

2. Why did Wells lose her teaching job?

_____

_____

_____

3. What happened after Wells bought part of a newspaper?

_____

_____

_____

travel	radio	photographs	African
newspapers	reporter	affect	

1. Choose the word from the word box above that best matches each definition. Write the word on the line below.

A. _____ having to do with or coming from Africa

B. _____ printed papers that tell what is happening in the world

C. _____ pictures that are taken with a camera

D. _____ to go to a different place

E. _____ a box that lets you hear music and sounds from far away

F. _____ a person who finds out what's happening and tells about it

G. _____ to change the way a person thinks about something

2. Fill in the blanks in the sentences below. Choose the word from the word box that completes each sentence.

A. The _____ showed how the new rock band looked.

B. I heard on the _____ that a storm was coming.

C. The heat in summer can _____ how fast I run.

D. The _____ writes about sports for our school newspaper.

E. One of our town's _____ printed a story about why the school's roof leaks.

F. The art in the library came from many _____ countries.

G. Our team needs to _____ a long way to be in the big game.

How the News Gets to You

1. Use the chart to help you remember what you read. On the lines, write *Reporters* if a choice describes what reporters do, *Photographers* if a choice describes what photographers do, or *Both* if a choice describes what both do.

Reporters, Photographers, or Both?

_____ **A.** take pictures of things that are happening

_____ **B.** affect how people think about new stories

_____ **C.** find out who, what, why, when, where, and how something happened

_____ **D.** talk to people to learn facts about a story

_____ **E.** show newspaper readers the *who* and *where* of the news

_____ **F.** write about the news

_____ **G.** help readers understand the news

_____ **H.** go where the news happens

2. Tell how you can use news stories and photographs together to learn about the news.

_____

_____

_____

_____

3. What are two differences between reading a story in a newspaper and watching it on TV news?

_____

_____

_____

_____

4. Tell about three ways the news can affect people's lives.

_____

_____

_____

_____

From Book to Movie

Many movies are based on books, such as the movie *Holes*.

Fast Facts

- The movie *The Outsiders*, which was based on a novel, was released twice: in 1983 and in 2005.

- The 2005 movie of *The Outsiders* is 22 minutes longer than the first movie.

- More than 100 movies have been made of Stephen King's books.

Making Movies

You've probably seen many movies, so you know that movies can be about many different things. Sometimes writers[20] create an idea for a movie. At other times, ideas for movies come from books.[35]

Any kind of book can be used to make a movie. Some books may tell stories the writer created. Others may be about real people and places.[62]

When a movie is based on a book, movie-makers decide how closely to follow the book. They decide how the people[84] and places in the book will look and which parts of the story they will show.[100]

KEY NOTES

Making Movies   What are some things movie-makers have to decide before they make a movie?

_____

_____

From Book to Movie

The book and movie called *The Lord of the Rings* showed a fantasy world.

Fast Facts

- The *Lord of the Rings* movies were shot in about 100 different places.

- The three *Lord of the Rings* movies cost about $270 million to make.

- A book was written about making the *Lord of the Rings* movies.

Making Fantasy Real

Some movies are based on fantasy books. In fantasy books, writers imagine a world of people and places that are[23] not real. It is the job of the movie-makers to show the world that the writer imagined.[41]

When the three *Lord of the Rings* books were made into movies, it took about 300 different sets to show the fantasy[63] world the writer had imagined. Although the books were more than 1,000 pages long, the three movies ran for only about[84] 11 hours. That means that the movie-makers had to show only the most important parts of the books.[103]

KEY NOTES

Making Fantasy Real

What are fantasy books?

_____

_____

From Book to Movie

Actors show people's thoughts.

Fast Facts

- In its first year, more than 2,500,000 copies of *To Kill a Mockingbird* were sold.

- *To Kill a Mockingbird* is the only book the writer Harper Lee ever published.

- The book gets its name from a person's warning: "It's a sin to kill a mockingbird."

Showing Ideas and Feelings

Writers tell what people are thinking. However, when books are turned into movies, actors must show people's thoughts.[22]

The book *To Kill a Mockingbird*, which was written by Harper Lee, was about a town in which white people were[43] unfair to African Americans. *To Kill a Mockingbird* was made into a movie in 1962.[58]

In her book, Harper Lee told how some white people in a town felt about African Americans. In the movie, actors[79] showed these feelings. The difference between the book and the movie is that the book told about unfairness while the movie showed it.[102]

KEY NOTES

Showing Ideas and Feelings   What is the difference between telling about people's thoughts and showing them?

_____

_____

From Book to Movie

Movies make comic book characters look real.

Fast Facts

- In 1952, Batman® and Superman® teamed up in a comic book.

- *Batman* was made into a TV show in the 1960s.

- The movie *Batman* made $251 million in the United States when it came out in 1989.

From Comics to Movies

Many people love reading about brave comic book characters, like Batman. The first Batman comic book was[21] printed in 1939. Since then, many movies have been made about this comic book character.[36]

The difference between comic books and movies is that movies show comic book characters as living people, not[54] drawings on a page. Actors can show more feelings than drawings can. Movies can also show actors doing things that[74] look real, like Batman speeding through the air in a flying car. Comic books, though, cost less and can be read at any time and anywhere.[100]

KEY NOTES

From Comics to Movies
How are comic books different from movies?

_____

_____

From Book to Movie

Making Movies

1. Another good name for "Making Movies" is _____

    a. "On the Screen."
    b. "Making Movies From Books."
    c. "How to Make Movies."
    d. "Making Books From Movies."

2. What are two kinds of books that can be used to make movies?

_____

_____

_____

3. In this reading, to *decide* means _____

_____

_____

_____

Making Fantasy Real

1. "Making Fantasy Real" is MAINLY about _____

    a. how to turn a fantasy book into a movie.
    b. why the *Lord of the Rings* books were written.
    c. how fantasy books are imagined.
    d. why the movie-makers made the *Lord of the Rings* movies.

2. What did the movie-makers decide before they made the *Lord of the Rings* movies?

    a. how to make the movies longer
    b. how to show the world that the writer imagined
    c. how to film all parts of the books
    d. how to imagine the people and places in the movies

3. How do you think movie-makers decide what to include in a movie made from a book?

_____

_____

_____

Showing Ideas and Feelings

1. Another good name for "Showing Ideas and Feelings" is _____

    a. "A Book and a Movie About Unfairness."
    b. "Filming *To Kill a Mockingbird.*"
    c. "Fairness and Unfairness in the Movies."
    d. "The Difference Between Showing and Telling."

2. *To Kill a Mockingbird* tells about _____

    a. what the African Americans liked about the town.
    b. how hard it is to make a movie from a book.
    c. why it is wrong to kill mockingbirds.
    d. how unfair some white people were to African Americans.

3. What is the main idea of this reading?

_____

_____

_____

From Comics to Movies

1. "From Comics to Movies" is MAINLY about _____

    a. the first Batman comic book.
    b. why so many Batman movies have been made.
    c. the differences between comics and movies.
    d. why people like reading and seeing Batman.

2. What are comic book characters?

_____

_____

_____

3. What can movies show that comics cannot?

_____

_____

_____

movie	decide	fantasy	imagine
mockingbird	African	comics	characters

1. Choose the word from the word box above that best matches each definition. Write the word on the line below.

   A. _____ having to do with or coming from Africa

   B. _____ people in books, movies, or plays

   C. _____ a kind of bird; it sings the songs of other birds

   D. _____ relating to stories that are told with drawings

   E. _____ a story that is told with moving pictures

   F. _____ to create stories or ideas in your mind

   G. _____ a kind of story that has places and characters that are not real

   H. _____ to make up your mind about something

2. Fill in the blanks in the sentences below. Choose the word from the word box that completes each sentence.

   A. I like to watch a _____ with teens who solve problems.

   B. A _____ is a kind of bird that sings the songs of other birds.

   C. Mara can't _____ which movie to see because they both sound good.

   D. Batman was first created for the _____.

   E. I like to read _____ books about strange worlds in space.

   F. Many _____ American families live in New York.

   G. Luis tried to _____ how his new home might look.

   H. The _____ of Batman and Robin try to keep people safe.

From Book to Movie

1. Use the idea web to help you remember what you read. In each box, write the main idea of that reading.

Making Movies

_____

_____

_____

_____

Making Fantasy Real

_____

_____

_____

_____

From Book to Movie

Showing Ideas and Feelings

_____

_____

_____

_____

From Comics to Movies

_____

_____

_____

_____

2. What are three things movie-makers have to think about when they want to make a movie from a book or comic book?

_____

_____

_____

_____

3. What are two differences between reading a story and seeing the same story in a movie?

_____

_____

_____

_____

4. Choose a book, story, or comic book that you think could be made into a movie. Which parts of the story and which characters would you include in the movie? Explain your choices.

_____

_____

_____

_____

Do Animals Talk?

Grizzly bears signal each other with tree marks.

Fast Facts

- A bark is a sound a dog makes to communicate to people or other animals.

- The brightness of a bird's feathers and the size of a bull's horns send information to other birds and bulls.

- Lizards communicate by moving their bodies.

How Animals Communicate

Animals don't talk, but they do communicate. When you communicate, you give information to others. Animals have[20] ways of communicating that are different from the ways people use. When your friend talks to you, your friend uses[40] language to communicate information. In a language, each word means something.[51]

Animals do not use words. Instead, they use sounds and signals. Birds sing and move their wings. Some animals, like[71] dogs, move their tails. Other animals communicate by moving their bodies in other ways. Some animals leave signs for other[91] animals to find. For example, bears scratch trees with their claws. Different sounds and signals help animals communicate with each other.[112]

KEY NOTES

How Animals Communicate

What is communication?

_____

_____

Do Animals Talk?

These honeybees are doing the round dance.

Fast Facts

- Honeybees dance differently during the day than after dark.

- Other kinds of bees, like bumblebees, also communicate by dancing.

- The kind of dance the honeybee does—round or waggle—tells how far away the nectar is.

The Honeybee Dance

One way honeybees communicate with each other is by dancing. Honeybees need the nectar in flowers to live. When[22] they find nectar, honeybees fly home to tell other bees where to find flowers with nectar. Their special dance tells the other honeybees where the flowers are.[49]

A honeybee that finds nectar moves its wings very fast when it dances. The bee moves in a shape that looks like the[72] number 8. The bee does the dance many times. How long the dance lasts tells the other bees how far away the flowers are.[96] After the dance, the other bees know just where to find the flowers with nectar.[111]

KEY NOTES

The Honeybee Dance
How do honeybees communicate with each other?

_____

_____

Do Animals Talk?

Humpback whales sing to communicate with each other.

Fast Facts

- Humpback whales signal each other when they jump high out of the water and crash back down.

- Laws were passed to keep humpbacks from being hunted too much.

- The low sounds made by blue whales are the loudest sounds made by any animal.

Whales

Whales communicate with each other by singing. Different kinds of whales sing different songs. Whales in[17] different parts of the world sing different songs, too. When a whale sings, people can sometimes hear the sound. People[37] near a singing whale might also feel the water move from the sound.[50]

The whales that sing the most are called humpbacks. Humpbacks make many different sounds and put these[67] sounds together in many different ways. When most kinds of whales communicate with each other, their songs are short.[86] Humpbacks, though, can sing for a long time. A humpback whale can sing for 20 minutes at a time. Some humpback whale songs are love songs.[112]

KEY NOTES

Whales

How do humpback whales communicate with each other?

_____

_____

Do Animals Talk?

Prairie dogs call out to other prairie dogs.

Fast Facts

- Some animals signal danger by making their tails straight as they run away.

- Some animals stay very still when they see danger.

- Prairie dogs communicate with each other by using "hello" or "danger" calls.

Danger Signals

People have danger signals to tell each other to be careful. Signs at train crossings and stop signs keep people from danger. Animals have danger signals, too.[29]

Some animals make sounds that tell other animals to be careful. The danger calls of many small birds sound the[49] same and communicate that all of the birds in an area should be careful.[63]

When prairie dogs think there is danger, they call to each other in a certain way. The danger might be bigger animals[85] that want to catch the prairie dogs and eat them. Their call tells other prairie dogs that they should be careful because they might be in danger.[112]

KEY NOTES

Danger Signals
How do people and animals use danger signals?

_____

_____

Do Animals Talk?

How Animals Communicate

1. "How Animals Communicate" is MAINLY about _____

    a. words animals can learn.
    b. how animals communicate.
    c. how animals understand people.
    d. how people communicate with animals.

2. How do animals communicate?

_____

_____

_____

3. How do animals and people communicate differently?

_____

_____

_____

The Honeybee Dance

1. Why do honeybees dance?

    a. to tell where the honey is
    b. to communicate with other animals
    c. to tell other bees how to get home
    d. to communicate with one another

2. How do honeybees dance?

_____

_____

_____

3. Why is the honeybee dance helpful to other honeybees?

_____

_____

_____

Whales

1. Another good name for "Whales" is _____

   a. "How Whales Communicate."
   b. "Different Kinds of Whales."
   c. "Humpback Whales."
   d. "Songs You Can't Hear."

2. Retell three facts you learned in "Whales."

_____

_____

_____

3. What kind of songs do whales sing?

    a. songs that communicate with many kinds of whales

    b. songs to make the water move

    c. songs that are short, long, or love songs

    d. songs that are all the same

Danger Signals

1. The main idea of "Danger Signals" is that _____

    a. signs at train crossings keep people safe.

    b. animals need humans to keep them safe.

    c. people and animals use danger signals to keep them safe.

    d. all animals use the same sounds to keep them safe.

2. Other prairie dogs know there is danger because _____

    a. they hear another prairie dog's call.

    b. they hear different kinds of animal calls.

    c. they see another prairie dog dance.

    d. they see other prairie dogs forming a big group.

3. Why do some animals use danger signals?

_____

_____

_____

communicate	information	language	honeybee	nectar
humpback	danger	signals	prairie	

1. Choose the word from the word box above that best matches each definition. Write the word on the line below.

A. _____ to give someone information

B. _____ a kind of insect that finds food in flowers

C. _____ words, signs, or movements that give information

D. _____ a kind of large whale that sings

E. _____ facts about something

F. _____ something that may hurt someone

G. _____ something that plants make that bees like to eat

H. _____ an area of open land where high grass grows

I. _____ words or other signs that people use to communicate

2. Fill in the blanks in the sentences below. Choose the word from the word box that completes each sentence.

A. Leah got _____ from a book about how to train her dog.

B. _____ whales can sing to each other over long distances.

C. The _____ landed on all of the flowers in the garden.

D. _____ helps people talk about their ideas.

E. Many animals _____ with each other by making sounds.

F. Dogs wag their tails as _____ that they are happy.

G. People can be in _____ when they are outside in bad weather.

H. Many animals live in the high grass of the _____.

I. Honeybees like to eat the _____ in flowers.

103

Do Animals Talk?

1. Use the idea web to help you remember what you read. In each box, write the main idea of that reading.

How Animals
Communicate

_____

_____

_____

_____

The Honeybee Dance

_____

_____

_____

**Do Animals
Talk?**

Whales

_____

_____

_____

_____

Danger Signals

_____

_____

_____

_____

2. Tell about two ways animals communicate with one another.

_____

_____

_____

_____

3. Tell about two reasons animals communicate with each other.

_____

_____

_____

_____

4. Why might animals want to warn each other about danger?

_____

_____

_____

_____

Water

Water is needed for all life on Earth.

Fast Facts

- Ice, steam, and drinking water are all forms of water.

- Clean water has no color, smell, or taste.

- Many people in the United States use power made from water.

Water in Your Life

You may not think that there is any water in your classroom. Yet water is always around you. Like animals and[25] plants, people's bodies are made up mostly of water. In fact, two-thirds of your body is water.[43]

Also like animals and plants, people need water to stay alive. People can't live for more than a few days without[64] water. They need to drink about 1 quart of water each day. In addition, many plants and animals live in water.[85]

People also use water to cook, grow food, and create power for light and heat. All life on Earth needs at least some water to stay alive.[112]

KEY NOTES

Water in Your Life
Why is water important to people, plants, and animals?

_____

_____

Water

Fresh water is found in rain, lakes, and rivers.

Fast Facts

- A small part of Earth's water comes from melting ice.

- In some countries, machines create drinking water by taking the salt out of water.

- In the United States, most of the fresh water is used for growing grass, filling pools, and washing cars.

Fresh Water and Salt Water

Almost three-quarters of Earth is water. However, much of Earth's water is the salt water in oceans. Fresh water can[26] be found in many lakes and rivers and under the ground.[37]

Although a little salt can make food taste good, people cannot drink salt water. Many animals and plants must also drink or live in fresh water.[63]

There is lots of fresh water on Earth, but it is not always where it is needed. In some places, little rain may fall for a[89] year or two. This means that everyone must use fresh water carefully so there will be enough for all life on Earth.[111]

KEY NOTES

Fresh Water and Salt Water

Why do people need fresh water?

_____

_____

Water

Rain is part of the water cycle.

Fast Facts

- On hot days, water vapor can make you feel sticky.

- Most water can be found under Earth's surface, in certain rocks, and in the ocean.

- Water also returns to the air through the loss of water by plants.

The Water Cycle

Rain that falls from the sky feels clean and new. It may be clean, but it is not new. The water in rain is really very old.[30] That's because water on Earth is used again and again. This use of water is called the water cycle.[49]

The water cycle starts when heat from the Sun helps to turn water in oceans and rivers into water vapor. Next, these[71] tiny drops of water vapor join to form clouds. Water then falls from the clouds as rain. Some water stays under the ground.[94] However, much of the water goes back into the oceans and rivers. Then, the water cycle starts over again.[113]

KEY NOTES

The Water Cycle

What is the water cycle?

_____

_____

Water

Water tests show if chemicals mixed with the water.

Fast Facts

- Some chemicals have no smell or taste, so do not drink water from streams or ponds that have not been filtered.

- Boiling water for 1 minute can help to make it safe to use.

- Laws have made it harder for factories and farms to let bad chemicals into water.

Clean Water

When you add water to a drink, you can see that it is easy to mix water with other things. Water can also mix with bad things, such as chemicals.[32]

Some factories and farms use chemicals. Some people also use chemicals to keep the grass on their lawns green.[51] Chemicals from factories, farms, and lawns can get into the water and hurt the plants and animals that live in it.[72] Chemicals can also hurt the people, plants, and animals that drink or use the water.[87]

Water should be cleaned before it is used. Water is filtered to get rid of bad chemicals. Filtered water is safe for drinking and cooking.[112]

KEY NOTES

Clean Water
Why is it important for water to be clean?

_____

_____

Water

Water in Your Life

1. "Water in Your Life" is MAINLY about _____

    a. all the water in a classroom.
    b. how important water is.
    c. why we drink water.
    d. how much water animals need.

2. Why do people need water?

_____

_____

_____

3. Name two things in or around your classroom that have water.

_____

_____

_____

Fresh Water and Salt Water

1. Another good name for "Fresh Water and Salt Water" is _____

    a. "Water in the Oceans."
    b. "Finding Drinking Water."
    c. "Living in Water."
    d. "Two Kinds of Water."

2. Compare where fresh water and salt water can be found.

_____

_____

_____

3. Why should people use fresh water carefully?

_____

_____

_____

The Water Cycle

1. What is the main idea of "The Water Cycle"?

    a. Water is used again and again.
    b. New water is made all the time.
    c. Water in rain is new water.
    d. Water from the sky is called water vapor.

2. Which shape BEST describes a cycle?

    a. a straight line
    b. a circle
    c. an angle
    d. a square

3. What are the steps in the water cycle?

_____

_____

_____

Clean Water

1. The main idea of "Clean Water" is that _____

    a. all water is safe.
    b. chemicals do not easily mix with water.
    c. water does not mix easily with other things.
    d. water must be clean to be safe to use.

2. How can water become unsafe to use?

_____

_____

_____

3. Why should bad chemicals be taken out of water?

_____

_____

_____

salt water	fresh water	cycle	vapor
clouds	factories	chemicals	filtered

1. Choose the word or words from the word box above that best match each definition. Write the word or words on the line below.

A. _____ the kind of water that is found in the oceans

B. _____ materials that can change other materials, for example, making water unsafe to drink

C. _____ tiny drops of water in the sky that join together

D. _____ the kind of water that is safe for people to drink

E. _____ a group of events that happen again and again

F. _____ large places where things are made

G. _____ when chemicals and other bad things are taken out of water

H. _____ tiny drops of water in the air

2. Fill in the blanks in the sentences below. Choose the word or words from the word box that complete each sentence.

A. In the water _____, rain falls and then it goes back into the air as water vapor.

B. Some _____ can make water unsafe to drink.

C. People can't drink the _____ in the oceans.

D. The _____ from the sink is safe to drink.

E. When water is heated, it turns into water _____ in the air.

F. _____ water has been cleaned, so it is safe to drink.

G. _____ have machines that can turn trees into paper.

H. Rain came down from the _____.

Water

1. Use the idea web to help you remember what you read. In each box, write the main idea of that reading.

Water in Your Life

_____

_____

_____

_____

Fresh Water and Salt Water

_____

_____

_____

_____

Water

The Water Cycle

_____

_____

_____

Clean Water

_____

_____

_____

2. Name three ways people use water every day.

_____

_____

_____

_____

3. Why is it important to keep water clean and to use it carefully?

_____

_____

_____

_____

4. Suppose there was another reading. Do you think it would be about rain or farms? Explain your choice.

_____

_____

_____

_____

Forces Around Us

Weights need force to move.

Fast Facts

- Your weight on every planet would be different from your weight on Earth.

- Weight is a force.

- A force will always act in a certain direction.

Push and Pull

Say you and a friend are playing with a sled. Your friend gets on the sled and asks you to move it. You can push or pull[30] the sled. When you push or pull it, you're using force. It's the use of force that lets you move the sled from place to place.[56]

To make the sled move faster, you'd need to use more force. If your friend doesn't weigh much, it won't take much[78] force to make the sled go faster. However, if your friend weighs a lot, it'll take more force to make the sled move faster.[102] No matter how fast something goes, it's force that makes it move.[114]

KEY NOTES

Push and Pull
What does force do?

_____

_____

Forces Around Us

Energy and force get work done.

Fast Facts

- The science of motion, force, and energy is called physics.

- When energy is stored, it is called potential energy.

- The energy of motion is called kinetic energy.

Energy and Work

When a force is used to move an object, it is called work. When you lift an object, such as a trash bag, you are doing work. Even if you lift a book, you are doing work.[40]

Work happens when you use force to make something happen. In order for the force to do the work, energy is used.[62]

You must have energy to do work. If you do a lot of work, you use a lot of energy. If you do just a little work, you don't[91] use very much energy. You get energy from food. Cars get energy from gas. It takes energy for work to be done.[113]

KEY NOTES

Energy and Work
What two things are needed for work?

_____

_____

Forces Around Us

Jumping takes force to go against gravity.

Fast Facts

- The force of gravity was discovered by Isaac Newton.

- The name of the unit used to measure force is the newton.

- The highest jump ever made by an insect was 28 inches high.

Up and Down

You may be able to jump, but you cannot jump 10 feet high. Gravity holds you down. Gravity is the force that pulls us back to Earth.[30]

You can, however, throw a ball 10 feet high. It doesn't take much force to toss a ball that high because a ball doesn't have much mass. It takes less force to move things with less mass.[67]

You have more mass than a ball. That's why it takes more force for you to jump 10 feet high than it takes to toss a ball[94] 10 feet high. Moving something with a lot of mass against the force of gravity takes a lot of energy.[114]

KEY NOTES

Up and Down
What does gravity do?

_____

_____

Forces Around Us

Ice is smooth so there is very little friction.

Fast Facts

- One type of friction is called sliding friction, such as sliding a book across a desk.

- Friction keeps bicycle wheels on the road.

- A sport in which you want little friction is ice-skating—with little friction between skate and ice you move faster.

Smooth and Rough

If you have ever tried to move an object such as a heavy desk, you know about friction. A heavy desk is hard[26] to drag over something that is rough, such as a rug. The desk does not move easily because it rubs against the rug. The[50] force that makes it hard to drag one thing over another is called friction.[64]

A heavy desk is easy to move over a slick floor. That is because there is less friction between objects and smooth[86] surfaces. There is more friction between objects and rough surfaces, such as a rug. If there is less friction, it is easier to move something.[111]

KEY NOTES

Smooth and Rough
What is friction?

_____

_____

Forces Around Us

Push and Pull

1. What can happen when you use force?

    a. You can find a sled.
    b. You can make something move.
    c. You can have fun with your friend.
    d. You can go from place to place.

2. Retell two facts you learned in "Push and Pull."

_____

_____

_____

3. In this reading *force* means _____

    a. moving something fast.
    b. moving something slow.
    c. the power or strength something has.
    d. playing a joke on someone.

Energy and Work

1. Another good name for "Energy and Work" is _____

    a. "What Is Force?"
    b. "Moving Trash Bags."
    c. "How Work Happens."
    d. "Making Energy."

2. When does work happen?

_____

_____

_____

3. Why did the author write "Energy and Work"?

    a. to give readers information about finding work
    b. to explain how energy is used to do work
    c. to compare energy and work
    d. to explain how cars get energy

Up and Down

1. What is "Up and Down" MAINLY about?

    a. how much mass a person has
    b. what the different forces are
    c. why people can jump 10 feet high
    d. how gravity works

2. What is gravity?

_____

_____

_____

3. Why can a person throw a ball 10 feet high but not be able to jump 10 feet high?

_____

_____

_____

Smooth and Rough

1. Friction is the force that _____

    a. makes it hard to drag one thing over another.

    b. keeps you from jumping high in the air.

    c. tells you when something is rough or smooth.

    d. gives you energy to move things.

2. Why is it easier to move something over a smooth surface than over a rough surface?

_____

_____

_____

3. What is the main idea of "Smooth and Rough"?

    a. how to move a heavy chair

    b. what friction does

    c. what is good about slick floors

    d. why rugs are rough surfaces

gravity	energy	force	object
friction	mass	rough	weigh

1. Choose the word from the word box above that best matches each definition. Write the word on the line below.

A. _____ to measure a thing or a person

B. _____ having an uneven surface

C. _____ an amount of matter

D. _____ something that can be seen or touched

E. _____ the force that is on an object

F. _____ the power or strength something has

G. _____ power

H. _____ what is created when two surfaces rub together

2. Fill in the blanks in the sentences below. Choose the word from the word box that completes each sentence.

A. The rug had a very _____ surface.

B. Sara had to _____ her dog.

C. It takes a lot of _____ to run to the school.

D. That _____ was the last to be packed.

E. She used great _____ to push the chair.

F. How much _____ do you think the ball has?

G. Pushing the box over the rug created _____.

H. _____ made it hard to keep the ball in the air.

Forces Around Us

1. Use the idea web to help you remember what you read. In each box, write the main idea of that reading.

Push and Pull

_____

_____

_____

Energy and Work

_____

_____

_____

Forces Around Us

Up and Down

_____

_____

_____

Smooth and Rough

_____

_____

_____

2. What was something new that you learned from reading about the forces around us?

_____

_____

_____

_____

3. Write a question you would like to ask the teacher about the forces around us.

_____

_____

_____

_____

4. Tell about something that you have noticed happening that you understand better now that you have read about the forces around us.

_____

_____

_____

_____

Popular Foods in the United States

Ice-cream cones are very popular.

Fast Facts

- About 13 quarts of ice cream are made every year for every person in the United States.

- Americans buy about $20 billion of ice cream every year.

- About 98 percent of all U.S. families buy ice cream.

Foods That People Love

It seems that popular foods like ice-cream cones and hot dogs have always been around. However, many popular foods[24] were first made when people wanted something that didn't take much time to make or eat. Many of these foods can be[46] eaten while standing up or while doing something else, like walking or watching TV. Some popular foods were made to solve a problem.[69]

Ice-cream cones, for example, were first made at the World's Fair in 1904. When an ice-cream seller ran out of[91] dishes, he solved his problem by taking a waffle, rolling it into a cone, and scooping ice cream into it. People loved eating waffles with ice cream, and a popular food was born.[124]

KEY NOTES

Foods That People Love
What does *popular* mean in this reading?

_____

_____

Popular Foods in the United States

Pizza uses flat bread and toppings.

Fast Facts

- The world's largest pizza order was for 13,386 pizzas.

- The first pizza store used an oven that was heated with lava from a local volcano.

- In the United States, more pizza is eaten during Super Bowl week than during any other week.

Pizza

Although pizza was first made in Italy, people in the Middle East were eating flat bread hundreds of years before[21] pizza was first made. Like pizza, the Middle Eastern bread did not rise or puff up, and it was topped with oil and spices.[45]

Flat bread became pizza in Italy in the late 1800s when a cook wanted to please the Italian king and queen. He wanted[68] to make a food that had the red, white, and green colors of the Italian flag, so he put red sauce, white cheese, and green herbs[94] on flat bread. When Italians came to the United States, they began making pizza in this country. Today, pizza is made around the world with many different toppings.[122]

KEY NOTES

Pizza

What is flat bread? Where was it first made?

_____

_____

Popular Foods in the United States

Many hot dogs are eaten outside.

Fast Facts

- In 2004, a total of 837 million packs of hot dogs were sold.

- In 2005, the winner of a New York hot-dog-eating contest ate 49 hot dogs in 12 minutes.

- Americans ate more than 27 million hot dogs at major-league baseball parks in 2005.

Hot Dogs

In about the year 900 B.C., Greek people were eating a food that was like a hot dog. However, people in Germany say that[26] the hot dogs that are popular today were first eaten there in 1487. They are called hot dogs because they look like a popular[50] little dog some Germans brought to the United States.[59]

In the United States, hot dogs were served to large numbers of people at a fair that was held in 1893. Many people[82] liked the food because it was both easy to eat and low in cost. That same year, hot dogs began to be served widely at ball[108] games. Today, hot dogs are one of the most popular foods in the United States.[123]

KEY NOTES

Hot Dogs
Why do people in the United States like hot dogs?

_____

_____

Popular Foods in the United States

There are many different kinds of tacos.

Fast Facts

- The largest taco was more than 35 feet tall and weighed 1,654 pounds.

- In Mexico, tacos are sometimes used as spoons to scoop up food.

- In Mexico, tacos are usually eaten in the morning or at night, not during the day.

Tacos

People have been eating tacos in North America for hundreds of years. In Mexico today, tacos are eaten the same[21] way sandwiches are eaten in the United States. People wrap meat, cheese, or other fillings in bread or a corn cake and eat their tacos while they walk or do other things.[53]

Also like sandwiches, tacos are filled with foods that are popular in different places. In the United States, tacos are[73] often filled with meat and cheese. In Mexico, though, tacos are filled with foods that are popular in certain areas. Near[94] the sea, for example, tacos are often filled with fish. In areas where cows are raised, tacos are often filled with beef. Tacos can even be filled with shark fins.[124]

KEY NOTES

Tacos

What are tacos?

_____

_____

Popular Foods in the United States

Foods That People Love

1. Many popular foods were created when people _____

    a. didn't have something they needed.
    b. wanted to eat something quickly.
    c. needed to solve a problem.
    d. all of the above

2. How are the two popular foods in this reading alike?

    a. They are both cold and sweet.
    b. They were both created at the World's Fair.
    c. They are both served on plates.
    d. They can be eaten while people do other things.

3. How were ice-cream cones created?

_____

_____

_____

Pizza

1. This reading is MAINLY about _____

    a. how pizza began.
    b. pizza toppings.
    c. Italians coming to the United States.
    d. flat breads around the world.

2. Why did the Italian cook make the pizza red, white, and green?

    a. so he didn't have to put cheese on the pizza
    b. because pizza was always made with those colors
    c. so the pizza would look like the Italian flag
    d. because he wanted to use foods the queen liked

3. Tell how pizza was first made.

_____

_____

_____

Hot Dogs

1. This reading is MAINLY about _____

    a. the history of hot dogs.
    b. why the Greeks made hot dogs.
    c. the kinds of hot dogs that were made.
    d. where hot dogs were first made.

2. German people called the food a hot dog because hot dogs _____

    a. were served when they were very hot.
    b. looked like a popular little dog.
    c. had once been served only to dogs.
    d. is an easy name to remember.

3. How did hot dogs become popular in the United States?

_____

_____

_____

Tacos

1. Where were tacos first made?

    a. in North America
    b. near the sea
    c. in places where there was meat
    d. in the United States

2. Tacos in Mexico are like sandwiches in the United States because both foods _____

    a. can be made with different fillings.
    b. can be eaten while people do other things.
    c. are very popular.
    d. all of the above

3. Why are taco fillings different in different areas of Mexico?

_____

_____

_____

popular	waffle	pizza	Italy
Germany	taco	Mexico	sandwich

1. Choose the word from the word box above that best matches each definition. Write the word on the line below.

A. _____ the country where pizza was first made

B. _____ when many people like something

C. _____ a popular food in Mexico that can have many different fillings

D. _____ a country to the south of the United States

E. _____ a food that can be eaten in the morning and can hold ice cream

F. _____ the country where hot dogs first became popular

G. _____ a flat bread that can have many different toppings

H. _____ a popular food in the United States that can have many different fillings

2. Fill in the blanks in the sentences below. Choose the word from the word box that completes each sentence.

A. I like slices of _____ that have lots of cheese.

B. _____ is one of the countries in North America.

C. People in _____ say that hot dogs were first eaten there in 1487.

D. Pizza was first made in _____.

E. In the United States, people usually make a _____ with two slices of bread.

F. Pizza and hot dogs are both _____ foods in the United States.

G. When an ice-cream seller ran out of dishes, he put ice cream in a _____.

H. A _____ is made with more kinds of fillings in Mexico than in the United States.

Popular Foods in the United States

1. Use the idea web to help you remember what you read. In each box, write the main idea of that reading.

Foods That People Love

_____

_____

_____

_____

Pizza

_____

_____

_____

_____

Popular Foods

Hot Dogs

_____

_____

_____

_____

Tacos

_____

_____

_____

_____

2. Choose two popular foods you read about in this topic. Tell how they are alike.

_____

_____

_____

_____

3. Choose two other popular foods you read about and tell how they are different.

_____

_____

_____

_____

4. Choose a kind of popular food that you did not read about in this topic. Tell why you like it and why you think it is popular.

_____

_____

_____

_____

Dance

People of ancient Greece enjoyed dance.

Fast Facts

- In ancient Egypt, sometimes dancers were hired to entertain at dinner parties.

- There were more than 200 ancient Greek dances.

- Most ancient Greek dances were done in a circle.

Dance Long Ago

Just as they do today, people long ago loved to dance. In Egypt, men and women might dance for fun. Men and [25] women also danced at important times. They danced to ask for the gods' help. [39]

Some of the most important dances were done when a person died. The Egyptian people thought special dances were important to help the person who died go to the afterlife. [69]

Long ago, the Greek people liked to dance because they thought dancing was good for the body and mind. Some [89] Greek dances were for men, others for women. Today, men and women dance together, but women dance in a slow and pretty way. Dance is still an important part of Greek life. [121]

KEY NOTES

Dance Long Ago
Why did Greek people like to dance long ago?

_____

_____

Dance

In some African dances, dancers jump into the air.

Fast Facts

- Drums are the most important instrument for African dance.

- In Mali, carvings of wild animals are carried as part of some dances.

- In a dance done in South Africa, the dancers wear work boots.

African Dances

Dance is a part of life in places in Africa. Dances may be done just for fun. They may also be part of a large event.[28]

Some African dances are done to help crops grow, or bring luck. For example, people might dance to bring good[48] luck in hunting for animals. In West Africa, dances tell stories about hunts that have already taken place.[66]

Some East African dances are contests that test people's skills. In one dance, young men leap into the air from the[87] ground to show how high they can jump. Another dance is a contest in which people dance with a cup of water on[110] their heads. The person who doesn't spill any water wins the contest.[122]

KEY NOTES

African Dances

What are two reasons for African dances?

_____

_____

Dance

Tap dance gets its name from the sounds made when the shoes hit the floor.

Fast Facts

- Tap dance used to be called flat-footed dancing.
- Some tap dancers can jump 10 feet and land in a split.
- The largest tap dance had 6,952 dancers.

Tap Dance

Tap dance is a kind of modern American dance. As tap dancers dance, they make tapping sounds as their shoes strike the floor.[25]

Tap dancing comes from several other dance forms. Tap has some African dance in it, as well as some English[45] clog dancing. Early tap dancers had shoes or boots with hard bottoms that made loud sounds as they danced. Other dancers[66] wore special shoes that made loud sounds. Many others danced with pennies attached to the bottoms of the shoes.[85] Modern tap shoes have plates, called taps, attached to the heel and toe.[98]

Before the 1830s, tap dance was done in the street. Today, people go to shows to watch the dances and hear the tapping sounds.[122]

KEY NOTES

Tap Dance
How has tap dancing changed?

_____

_____

Dance

Some hip-hop steps are from tap dance.

Fast Facts

- Hip-hop music began in New York City.

- Music videos helped to spread hip-hop music and dance all over the world.

- The United States Postal Service has a stamp with a hip-hop dancer on it.

Hip-Hop

Hip-hop dances have steps with names like glide, float, pop and lock, and backspin. In the 1970s, hip-hop music was[21] called rap music. It began in the United States. People quickly created dances based on the strong beat of the music.[42]

In the 1970s, hip-hop dances were called break dances. Today, most people call it hip-hop dancing. Some of the steps[62] in hip-hop come from African dance, while other steps come from tap dance.[75]

Dancers take turns jumping, rolling, spinning, and stepping in hip-hop contests. They try to dance faster and[92] better than all the other dancers. They may even try to create some brand new hip-hop steps. People clap their hands for the dancers they think won the contest.[121]

KEY NOTES

Hip-Hop
What is hip-hop dance?

_____

_____

Dance

Dance Long Ago

1. Another good name for "Dance Long Ago" is _____

    a. "New Dances."
    b. "Dance Steps."
    c. "The Greek People."
    d. "Dance in the Past."

2. Why did the author write "Dance Long Ago"?

    a. to tell how dance is the same today as long ago
    b. to tell that men did not dance with women
    c. to tell how people danced long ago
    d. to tell how Greek dance is like Egyptian dance

3. Tell why dance was important to people long ago.

_____

_____

_____

African Dances

1. In this reading, the word *contest* means _____

_____

_____

_____

2. This reading is MAINLY about _____

    a. hunting dances.

    b. kinds of dances in Africa.

    c. jumping dances.

    d. war dances.

3. Explain your answer to question 2.

_____

_____

_____

Tap Dance

1. Why did the author write "Tap Dance"?

    a. to give readers information about tap dance

    b. to teach readers how to tap dance

    c. to tell how tap shoes are made

    d. to tell about the first tap dance

2. What is special about tap shoes?

_____

_____

_____

3. Where do people go to see tap dance?

_____

_____

_____

Hip-Hop

1. In this reading, *create* means _____

    a. to find something.
    b. to complete something.
    c. to make up something.
    d. to leave something.

2. Where did some hip-hop steps come from?

    a. dance contests
    b. music contests
    c. tap dances and African dance
    d. rap music

3. Explain your answer to question 2.

_____

_____

_____

create	Africa	Greek	contest
attached	Egypt	modern	music

1. Choose the word from the word box above that best matches each definition. Write the word on the line below.

A. _____ sounds people like to listen to

B. _____ a country of the world

C. _____ an event in which people try to do better than others

D. _____ when something is added to something else

E. _____ new and in the present

F. _____ a large continent

G. _____ the name of a group of people from Greece

H. _____ to make something new

2. Fill in the blanks in the sentences below. Choose the word from the word box that completes each sentence.

A. Sam and Dan _____ the sign to a pole.

B. The _____ made us want to dance.

C. Long ago, people in _____ danced when a person died.

D. In _____ times, we still like to learn about the past.

E. The _____ is to see who is the best dancer.

F. The _____ people thought dancing was good for the body and the mind.

G. You can see the jump dance in different places in _____.

H. The girls worked to _____ a new kind of dance.

Dance

1. Use the idea web to help you remember what you read. In each box, write the main idea of that reading.

Dance Long Ago

_____

_____

_____

_____

African Dances

_____

_____

_____

_____

Dance

Tap Dance

_____

_____

_____

Hip-Hop

_____

_____

_____

2. Write the most surprising thing you read about dance. Explain your choice.

_____

_____

_____

_____

3. Why do you think people enjoy dancing?

_____

_____

_____

_____

4. Which kind of dance that you read about would you be most interested in seeing? Why?

_____

_____

_____

_____

Wearable Art

Anyone can create wearable art.

Fast Facts

- One of the first wearable art shows in the United States was in 1946.

- Socks with bright designs, such as rainbow giraffes, are wearable art.

- Some well-known artists, such as Alexander Calder, have made jewelry that is wearable art.

What Is Wearable Art?

Sometimes the clothes we wear do more than just cover us—they are art. Wearable art may be old or new, and it may[28] be made with gems, pins, paper clips, or other things. This kind of art may be sewn or painted by an artist, someone you know, or even you.[56]

Artists create many kinds of wearable art. Some put gems on coats or shoes or paint pictures on shirts, scarves, or robes.[78] Some sew pictures on jeans or knit clothes in different colors. Some also put pins and beads on hats.[97]

Many people create wearable art so they have clothes that are different from everyone else's. Wearable art is made and worn by people around the world.[123]

KEY NOTES

What Is Wearable Art?

What things can be part of wearable art?

_____

_____

Wearable Art

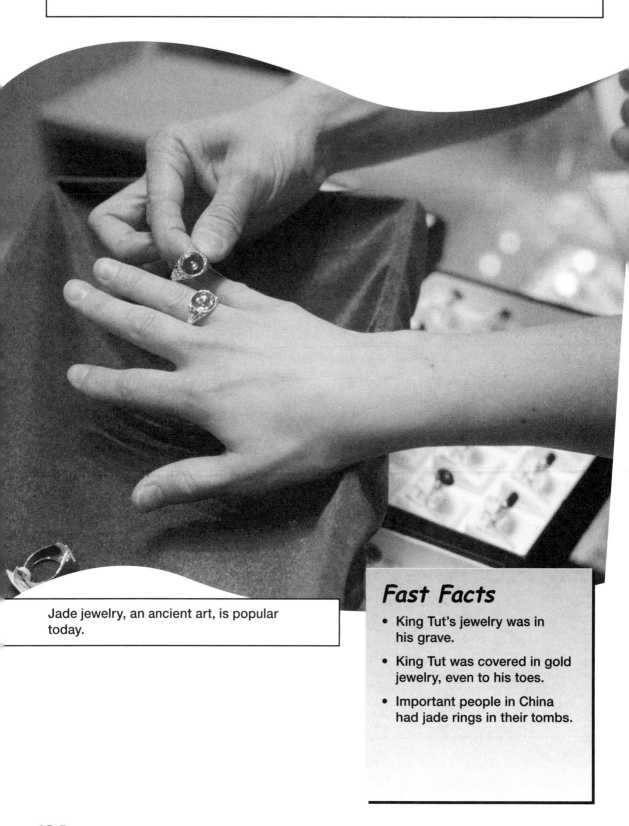

Jade jewelry, an ancient art, is popular today.

Fast Facts

- King Tut's jewelry was in his grave.

- King Tut was covered in gold jewelry, even to his toes.

- Important people in China had jade rings in their tombs.

Jewelry as Art

One kind of wearable art is jewelry, such as rings. Jewelry that is wearable art can be made from gold or[24] gemstones. It can also be made from things that are in the house. Some people like to make jewelry from paper clips or[47] safety pins. Rings can be made out of twigs or wire. Some people glue together seashells to make pins.[66]

Some wearable art jewelry was worn a long time ago. Today, in museums, we can see jewelry from King Tut's[86] tomb. We can also see jade jewelry that was worn by important people in China. Artists can study jewelry from[106] the past in museums and make new pieces based on what they have seen.[120]

KEY NOTES

Jewelry as Art

Why is some jewelry called wearable art?

_____

_____

Wearable Art

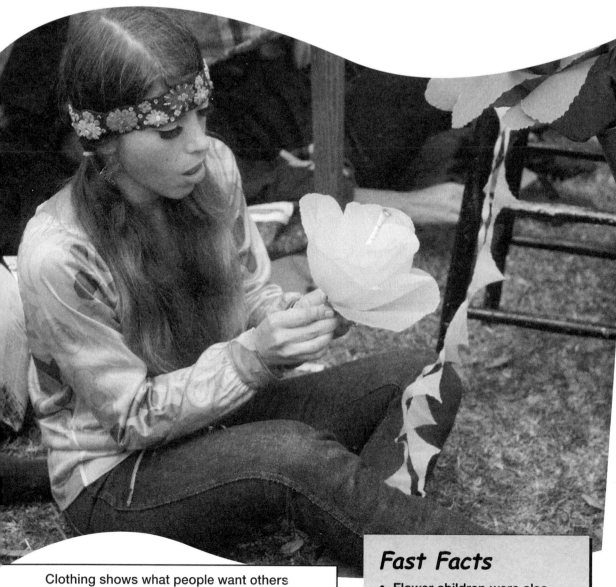

Clothing shows what people want others to know.

Fast Facts

- Flower children were also called hippies.

- Hippies used words such as *groovy* for something that was cool.

- Many hippies lived in San Francisco.

Flower Power

In the 1960s, many people thought their clothing should show their ideas. They thought that what they wore should[21] say something about them. Some people who wanted to show they were against war called their idea "flower power." These[41] people painted colorful flowers on their faces and clothes and wore flowers in their hair.[56]

Today, people like to show their ideas on T-shirts. They paint flowers, animals, and other colorful things on their[75] shirts and coats. They also wear sayings that mean something to them or names of brands they like. They wear what they[97] want other people to know about them. Wearable art can help people tell others what they think, what they like, and who they are.[121]

KEY NOTES

Flower Power
What was flower power?

_____

_____

Wearable Art

This dress by Jennifer Stern has beads added to flowers.

Fast Facts

- For one gown, Jennifer Stern spent more time at her computer than at her sewing machine.

- One coat took nearly 400 hours to create.

- One of Jennifer Stern's creations has been on the cover of a book.

An Artist of Wearable Art

Jennifer Stern is a sewing teacher. She is also an artist who makes wearable art. Stern uses a sewing machine to[26] make special dresses. She also uses computer software to make dresses that are colorful.[40]

After Stern makes a dress with her sewing machine, she uses computer software to draw flowers on the dress. Next,[60] she sews the colorful flower pictures onto the dress with her sewing machine. Finally, she adds beads of different colors to the flowers, sewing them on one at a time.[90]

Stern might use the same flowers that are on a dress and add them on a jacket to match the dress. She has also won contests for the wearable art she has made.[123]

KEY NOTES

An Artist of Wearable Art
What does Jennifer Stern do?

_____

_____

Wearable Art

What Is Wearable Art?

1. The MAIN idea of "What Is Wearable Art?" is that _____

    a. art can be old or new.
    b. artists can add gems to shoes.
    c. clothes can be art.
    d. few people make wearable art.

2. Wearable art can _____

    a. be made by anyone.
    b. come from one part of the world.
    c. be made only by artists.
    d. be sold in stores.

3. Name two different kinds of wearable art.

_____

_____

_____

Jewelry as Art

1. The main idea of "Jewelry as Art" is that _____

    a. jewelry can be wearable art.
    b. paper clips can be made into jewelry.
    c. there is jewelry in King Tut's tomb.
    d. wearable art jewelry has been made for a long time.

2. Name three things that can be used to make wearable art jewelry.

_____

_____

_____

3. What can people learn from old wearable art jewelry?

_____

_____

_____

Flower Power

1. Another title for "Flower Power" could be _____

    a. "Art That Says Something."
    b. "T-shirts."
    c. "War."
    d. "Flowers People Wear."

2. How did some people in the 1960s show they were against war?

    a. They planted flowers.
    b. They told others about flowers.
    c. They wore jewelry.
    d. They wore flowers on their clothes and in their hair.

3. Why do people today wear clothes with sayings on them?

_____

_____

_____

An Artist of Wearable Art

1. What are two things Jennifer Stern uses to make wearable art?

_____

_____

_____

2. Another title for "An Artist of Wearable Art" could be _____

    a. "How to Use a Computer."
    b. "Who Is Jennifer Stern?"
    c. "Learn How to Sew."
    d. "Beads and Flowers."

3. Why is Jennifer Stern called a wearable art artist?

_____

_____

wearable	jewelry	computer	museum
flowers	artist	colorful	machine

1. Choose the word from the word box above that best matches each definition. Write the word on the line below.

A. _____ plants with blooms

B. _____ rings, earrings, and other things people wear to look beautiful

C. _____ a place to see art and other things

D. _____ a person who makes beautiful things

E. _____ something that can be put on

F. _____ something that does work that doesn't have to be done by hand

G. _____ something that stores numbers and words

H. _____ having many bright colors

2. Fill in the blanks in the sentences below. Choose the word from the word box that completes each sentence.

A. I can sew quickly by using a sewing _____.

B. Let's pick some roses or other kinds of _____.

C. Her _____ dress had many different reds and greens.

D. She uses a laptop _____ at work.

E. Shirts with pictures on them are a kind of _____ art.

F. The ring looked like one in the _____ that was worn by a king.

G. She likes rings and other kinds of _____.

H. My mother is an _____ who loves to paint.

Wearable Art

1. Use the idea web to help you remember what you read. In each box, write the main idea of that reading.

What Is Wearable Art?

_____
_____
_____
_____

Jewelry as Art

_____
_____
_____
_____

Wearable Art

Flower Power

_____
_____
_____
_____

An Artist of Wearable Art

_____
_____
_____
_____

2. Why do you think people like wearable art?

_____

_____

_____

_____

3. List two facts you learned about wearable art.

_____

_____

_____

_____

4. Tell about two pieces of wearable art that you have or that you have seen.

_____

_____

_____

_____

Acknowledgments

Photo Credits

Cover photos: (top) BananaStock/Punchstock; (bottom, L-R) Stockbyte Silver/Getty Images; Comstock Images/Punchstock; Digital Vision/Punchstock; Dave Bartruff/Digital Vision/Getty Images; **Page:** 8 Comstock Images/Jupiter Images; 10 Art Montes De Oca/Taxi/Getty Images; 12 © Joseph Sohm/Visions of America/Corbis. All Rights Reserved.; 14 Comstock Images/Jupiter Images; 22 Rue des Archives/The Granger Collection, NYC; 24 Betty Sederquist/Ambient Images; 26 PhotoDisc/Getty Images; 28, 140 © David Young-Wolff/PhotoEdit; 36 Library of Congress; 38 © Claro Cortes IV/Reuters/Corbis; 40 Spencer Grant/Photo Researchers, Inc.; 42 David Madison/Stone/Getty Images; 50 © David Grossman/The Image Works; 52 Anne Frank Fonds—Basel/Anne Frank House—Amsterdam/Getty Images; 54 The Great Fire of London, 1666 (print), Verschuier, Lieve (1630-86) (after)/Private Collection/The Bridgeman Art Library; 56 Corbis/Jupiter Images; 64 Merrill Education; 66 Prentice Hall School Division; 68 © Stockbyte/Corbis; 70 Schomburg Center/Art Resource, NY; 78 Buena Vista/The Kobal Collection; 80 Photofest; 82 © Bettmann/Corbis; 84 Jochen Tack/Peter Arnold, Inc.; 92 Mary McDonald/Nature Picture Library; 94 © Jimmy Lee/Shutterstock; 96 Wolcott Henry/National Geographic Image Collection; 98 © Jeff Gynane/Shutterstock; 106 © Robert W. Ginn/PhotoEdit; 108 Alan Smith/Stone/Getty Images; 110 Howard B. Bluestein/Photo Researchers Inc.; 112 © Frank Pedrick/The Image Works; 120 © Dana White/PhotoEdit; 122 © CLEO PHOTOGRAPHY/Photo Edit. All rights reserved.; 124 Stockbyte/Stockbyte Platinum/Getty Images; 126 Jamie Squire/AllSport Concepts/Getty Images; 134 © Michael Newman/PhotoEdit; 136 © Michael Newman/PhotoEdit; 138 © Spencer Grant/PhotoEdit; 148 Rèunion des Musèes Nationaux/Art Resource, NY; 150 Bruno De Hoques/Stone/Getty Images; 152 Tim Boyle/Getty Images; 154 Positive Reflections, Inc.; 162 Stockbyte/Stockbyte Platinum/Getty Images; 164 © age fotostock/SuperStock; 166 © Henry Diltz/Corbis/All Rights Reserved.; 168 Jennifer Stern

Text Credits

- Model T is a registered trademark of Ford Motor Company.
- *Anne Frank: The Diary of a Young Girl* (book). Copyright © 1991, 2001 by The Anne Frank-Fonds, Basel, Switzerland. English translation copyright © 1995, 2001 by Doubleday, a division of Random House, Inc. Photographs copyright © The Anne Frank-Fonds, Basel, Switzerland. Anne Frank Stichting. The diary entry that appears on the endpapers is copyright © The Anne Frank-Fonds, Basel, Switzerland. All Rights Reserved. Printed in the United States of America. March 1995.
- *The Diary of Anne Frank* (movie). Dir. George Stevens. © 1959 Twentieth Century Fox Film Corporation. © Renewed 1987 Twentieth Century Fox Film Corporation. All Rights Reserved. © 2004 Twentieth Century Fox Home Entertainment, Inc. All Rights Reserved.
- *Holes* (book) by Louis Sachar. Copyright © 1998 by Louis Sachar. Published by Dell Yearling, an imprint of Random House Children's Books, a division of Random House, Inc.
- *Holes* (movie). 2003. Copyright © Buena Vista Home Entertainment, Inc. and Walden Media LLC.
- *The Outsiders* (book) by S.E. Hinton. Published by the Penguin Group/Penguin Putnam Books for Young Readers. Copyright © S.E. Hinton, 1967. Copyright renewed S.E. Hinton, 1995. All rights reserved.
- *The Outsiders* (movie). 1983, 2005. *The Outsiders: The Complete Novel*, dir. Francis Ford Coppola. The Outsiders © 1983 Pony Boy Inc. Copyright © 1999 Warner Home Video;

The Outsiders: The Complete Novel and Supplementary Material Compilation © 2005 Zoetrope Corporation. Package Design © 2005 Warner Bros. Entertainment Inc. Distributed by Warner Home Video Inc., 4000 Warner Blvd., Burbank, CA 91522. All Rights Reserved.
- *The Lord of the Rings* (books): *The Fellowship of the Ring, The Two Towers, and The Return of the King* by J.R.R. Tolkien. 50th Anniversary One-Volume Edition. Boston: Houghton Mifflin Company: *The Fellowship of the Ring* (book). Copyright © 1954, 1965, 1966 by J.R.R. Tolkien. 1954 edition copyright © renewed by Christopher R. Tolkien, Michael H.R. Tolkien, John F.R. Tolkien and Priscilla M.A.R. Tolkien; 1965/1966 editions copyright renewed 1993, 1994 by Christopher R. Tolkien, John F.R. Tolkin and Priscilla M.A.R. Tolkien. *The Two Towers* (book). Copyright © 1954, 1965, 1966 by J.R.R. Tolkien. 1954 edition copyright © renewed by Christopher R. Tolkien, Michael H.R. Tolkien, John F.R. Tolkien and Priscilla M.A.R. Tolkien; 1965/1966 editions copyright renewed 1993, 1994 by Christopher R. Tolkien, John F.R. Tolkin and Priscilla M.A.R. Tolkien. *The Return of the King* (book). Copyright © 1955, 1965, 1966 by J.R.R. Tolkien. 1955 edition copyright © renewed by Christopher R. Tolkien, Michael H.R. Tolkien, John F.R. Tolkien and Priscilla M.A.R. Tolkien. 1965/1966 editions copyright renewed 1993, 1994 by Christopher R. Tolkien, John F.R. Tolkin and Priscilla M.A.R. Tolkien.
- *The Lord of the Rings* (movies) © 2001 New Line Productions, Inc.; © 2002 New Line Home Entertainment, Inc. *The Lord of the Rings*, the characters, names and places therein, TM The Saul Zaentz Company d/b/a Tolkien Enterprises under license to New Line Productions, Inc. All Rights Reserved. *The Lord of the Rings, The Two Towers*, the characters, names and places therein, TM The Saul Zaentz Company d/b/a Tolkien Enterprises under license to New Line Productions, Inc. All Rights Reserved. *The Lord of the Rings, The Return of the King*, the characters, names and places therein, TM The Saul Zaentz Company d/b/a Tolkien Enterprises under license to New Line Productions, Inc. All Rights Reserved.
- *To Kill a Mockingbird* (book) by Harper Lee. Copyright © 1960, renewed 1988 by Harper Lee. New York: HarperCollins/Harper Perennial/Modern Classics. Perennial Classics are published by Perennial, an imprint of HarperCollins Publishers.
- *To Kill a Mockingbird* (movie). Dir. Robert Mulligan. © 2005 Universal Studios. All Rights Reserved. 10 Universal City Plaza, Universal City, CA 91606.
- *Batman*® (comic book). Copyright © 2006 DC Comics. All rights reserved.
- *Superman*® (comic book). Copyright © 2006 DC Comics. All rights reserved.
- *Batman Begins* (movie). Dir. Christopher Nolan. Batman and all related characters and elements are trademarks of and © DC Comics. Copyright © 2005 Patalex III Productions Limited. Package Design and Supplementary Material Compilation © 2005 Warner Bros. Entertainment Inc. Distributed by Warner Home Video Inc.; 4000 Warner Blvd., Burbank, CA 91522. All Rights Reserved.

Staff Credits

Members of the AMP™ QReads™ team: Melania Benzinger, Karen Blonigen, Carol Bowling, Michelle Carlson, Kazuko Collins, Nancy Condon, Barbara Drewlo, Sue Gulsvig, Daren Hastings, Laura Henrichsen, Ruby Hogen-Chin, Julie Johnston, Mary Kaye Kuzma, Julie Maas, Daniel Milowski, Carrie O'Connor, Julie Theisen, Mary Verrill, Mike Vineski, Charmaine Whitman